For Cal—
With thanks for
listening —

love
Mary Ann

June 8, 1998

Wick Poetry Chapbook Series
Maggie Anderson, Editor

White Sustenance
Kat Snider Blackbird

Sleepwalking with Mayakovsky
Robert Brown

Sabishi: poems from japan
David Hassler

Rooms by the Sea
Mary Ann Samyn

ROOMS BY THE SEA

Mary Ann Samyn

Mary Ann Samyn

The Kent State University Press

Kent, Ohio, & London, England

© 1994 by Mary Ann Samyn
All rights reserved
Library of Congress Catalog Card Number 94-29383
ISBN 0-87338-514-4
Manufactured in the United States of America

The Wick Poetry Chapbook series is sponsored by the
Stan and Tom Wick Poetry Program and the Department
of English at Kent State University.

Library of Congress Cataloging-in-Publication Data
Samyn, Mary Ann 1970–
    Rooms by the Sea/Mary Ann Samyn.
        p.   cm. — (Wick poetry chapbook series)
    ISBN 0-87338-514-4 (pbk.: alk. paper) ∞
    I. Title. II. Series.
PS3569.A46695R66 1994
811'. 54—dc20   94-29383
                                                          CIP

British Library Cataloging-in-Publication data are available.

For my father

And for Ed—
a candle, an echo, a star

CONTENTS

ACKNOWLEDGMENTS

Grateful acknowledgment is made to the editors of the publications in which the following poems first appeared: "Heat," *The Laurel Review* 28.1 (Winter 1994); "October Breakdown," *Lullwater Review* 5.2 (Fall/Winter 1994); "Squall Line," *Mudfish* 7 (1993).

"First Things" and "Birds" are for Edward Haworth Hoeppner, for everything.

I would also like to thank Jennifer Parker for listening and Tom Andrews for his careful readings and encouragement.

KINDLING

My mother will appear like fire
below the burners, that quick twist
of gas. She will be that blue,
and there will be no turning her down.

Already my skin blisters as I burn
my thumb, watch as the water runs over it,
circles in the sink like her voice, the rush
in my ears, the hot and cold of her words.

Milk hardens in the pan,
brown, like my mother's face.
On the outside, the heat holds on,
turns the silver black, forms ridges,

the contours of her hands that curl
around my own until I disappear,
a doorknob beneath her palm,
her fingers listening for some click.

Soon she'll come up the walk,
and the trees will drop their leaves
around her, the yellows and oranges
drifting down among the branches,

sparking as they hit the ground.

I

Now that I have your heart by heart, I see.
—Louise Bogan, "Song for the Last Act"

CARRY OUT

In a moment's kindness, the nurses looked
the other way as we ate Chinese food

two nights before you could have died
but didn't. Your room smelled of hyacinths,

soy sauce, and antiseptic. We took turns
sitting in the one chair, then on the windowsill,

the foot of your bed, forgetting, if only for a minute,
where we were, who the patient was.

It was dark out, yet we left the curtains
open as though to keep the world

with us, the predictability of street lights,
the reassurance of cars braking.

Five flights up, there was a hum in the room,
a sound that was more than our voices

or the machines guarding you.
Its rhythm was like traffic in the distance,

like our hands taking turns, grasping yours.

FIVE A.M.

I enter through the basement,
walk past the cafeteria, slices

of pie wrapped in plastic, past rooms
with thick doors and small windows.

I ride up in the elevator. It shakes,
barely holding me, my limbs heavy,

my heart full, a bag of stones
I finger again and again.

On my father's floor I think
I hear the sound of cells calling,

fighting for their lives, and out
the window I see an ambulance,

strangely silent, nearing this place
where all the noise is internal.

The room is dark but my father
is awake, his body shining

like a fish those first few moments
on shore, caught yet still wet.

He has taken three showers
with the soap that makes him nearly

clean enough for their blades.
His chest heaves with the thought

of knives through him, the first drops
of blood like sprinkles on the sidewalk,

the surprise of thunder in the distance.
My ears strain and my eyes search

for his heart, valves and chambers.
Instead, I have only his hands,

useless tools I'd like to feel
beneath my palm, hold there.

Slowly the drugs pull at him
until his hand slackens in mine

and he slurs last instructions.
The light from the hall comes first,

then the men with their orders.
They lift him, the sheets falling

at the foot of the bed, cooling there.
I watch until they turn the corner.

OPEN HEART

On your chest the stitches swim,
thin black fish, flesh

like small mouths puckering.
Loose, cut from its wet sac,

your heart cries red
into an awkward gutter where

blood collects like rainwater.
And your ribs, lonesome

and tangled in wire, are a gate
now, swinging open,

letting something in.

THE GIFT

The surgeon came to you
like a god, spreading

your ribs, holding your heart
still while your blood

bloomed in his hands
like those flowers near the bed.

His finger moved through
the labyrinth of valves and chambers,

the light above him like stars
he pulled from the pocket

of his white coat and flung
there. He held the knife,

a gift, until finally he set your heart
down, pulling you back,

wreathing your ribs with wire.
Later he bent over you,

two fingers tracing the cut
again, feeling for some rough

spot in the weave, the cross-stitch
just visible as a signature.

COMING TO

Now someone else is lying in your bed
in the hospital where they opened you,

held your heart down. I drive past, remember
the days you spent in that place where you were

listening but not talking. There was a stillness
around you, water on the windows,

the heat that kept you warm but made us sick.
How different your living was then,

how measured. Now all that has moved off,
the sheets from your bed washed and used a hundred times,

the pillow holding other dim faces.
But you cannot remember the way we leaned

over you, looked for answers in the space
between your lips, in the words we were sure

were forming there. Yet we grieve and feel small,
hardly knowing where you have been,

where someone else is now.

HEAT

My father's in the basement pounding nails,
and the bird is singing in its dark cage

and no one can sleep with this new snow.
He is so far away it seems as if there is

no hammer, no wood, only his hands
and the nails, the sound drifting

up to me with the heat of the furnace.
I think the bird knows, whistling anxiously,

but everywhere the snow is heavy on us,
sending my father, restless, out of his bed,

into the basement, closer to the fire
and the wood and his tools. And we wait,

the bird and I, keep a vigil for him,
hearing the furnace click off, then on,

listening for his pounding hands, or his feet
on the stairs, resigned finally to this cold.

A SONG I AM LEARNING

If my father's voice is a river,
then sadness is its water.

I wade in, rocks
slippery beneath my feet.

I feel the current, slow,
deliberate over them.

If there is music here,
it is deep throated, a sighing

or a kind of prayer that speaks
of darkness, endings.

All around me it rises
up, lingers in the tall grasses

then circles back to find me,
water dripping from my arms,

pebbles in my hands.

I I

My mother remembers the agony of her womb
And the long years that seemed to promise more than this.
She says, "You do not love me,
You don't want me
You will go away."
      —Louise Bogan, "Betrothed"

MOTHER

Because we have no diagnosis, no words like *schizophrenia*, we are mostly silent. If anyone is sick my mother says, it is my father, my sisters, my brother, me.

*

When she is sad, my niece says that there is a stone in her heart.

*

Bedtime stories:

When her father died, my mother was two and her mother was pregnant with another child. My aunts say that it was cough medicine that finally stopped my mother's crying, made her sleep.

*

My mother is the stone in my heart.

*

At ten, my mother boarded a bus with her oldest sister. They rode until they reached a neighborhood she knew of as not-as good, but her sister pointed to a house, said "ours." My mother felt hungry from the long trip, sick from the sun through the windows. She knew that her father was dead and the money was gone. She thought of her brothers away at camp, wondered when they'd be home, how they'd know where to come.

*

Smoke curled from the chimney.
My mother pressed her cheek to the window,
watched the smoke blow away.

*

At high school socials, the nuns told her she was the smartest
girl, she should have danced with the smartest boy. At home
her sisters said the same thing, rolled her hair in the pink
curlers that poked her awake again and again. In the morning
the curls framed her face, tumbled down her back.

*

I imagine her small mouth
around the spoon, the cough syrup
replaced by her reflection, upside
down and strangely curved.

*

When she met my father, it was after Mass and they were
in the church basement. Seeing him there, she knew he was
good. When he knelt, she could feel him praying. When
he talked, he moved his hands, brown oars through deep
water.

*

When my mother goes away,
I can hear it in my father's voice,
as though he's lost something.

*

They were married in the morning. The reception was a brunch where there was no dancing. They drove my mother's car to New York City, and though she doesn't say this, I imagine other motorists saw my father's arm resting on the open window, saw my mother's long hair, a brown kite blowing.

*

The curls tumbled down her back.

*

My father took the bus to work, left the car for my mother. But she hardly moved it from the driveway, only going out to circle the neighborhood, praying one child fell asleep, the other didn't wake.

*

If my father's hands are brown oars,
my mother rides in the boat he rows.

*

When my mother said two were enough, then three, then four, her sisters said, what about seven, what about nine. She went to priests, but they talked of duty, faithfulness. They moved like black candles, their robes reaching to the floor, their awful tongues quivering.

*

My mother says the walls have ears. Be careful—even now they are listening.

*

When I was born, my mother was forty and she knew to worry. She was sitting on the front porch when she felt the pains, the familiar startle. But I was the easy one, born on a Sunday at dusk. It is a time of day we both love, the sun giving up the sky, the moon rising cool and white.

*

Now when she sees a bus,
she says she'd like to take it
anywhere. I imagine her riding
in a yellow school bus, rounding
the corner, wheeling
out of sight.

*

We sat on the dining-room floor and my mother watched while I named dolls. Again and again I asked her to pretend with me. Her hair was brown but I told her it was black and she was five and I was seven. I poured tea into the tiny blue cups, scolded her for spilling some on the saucer, promised to teach her what it meant to be a lady.

*

The moon is a ball of wax
my mother warms
in the palm of her hand.
She molds it, quarter,
half or whole.

*

When I was fourteen, she nearly died. She thought she had cancer, but she didn't mind, said dying was like forgetting. My father tried to give her a sleeping pill; she spit it out, kicked it under the counter. We stood back, blocked the kitchen doors, trapped her there.

*

My mother is broken.
But to whom can I tell this?
Not the nun the day I flunk
a math test, not my friends
whose mothers pack their lunches.

*

Some nights she said the walls had ears. I listened hard, but all I heard were the words she mumbled as she made dinner, the water she left running, swirling down the sink. If my mother was right, then our house was thick with talking, even the smoke from the chimney, the way it curled above us, was a sign. She said it was a tongue and we were all anointed.

*

She felt sick from the sun through the windows.

*

Three years ago, when my father and I moved to another house, my mother was in Florida. I imagined she could hear the door closing a thousand miles away. A week later I wrote a poem about a stone. I said it was my mother's heart the day we left, the day we slammed the door. But I knew this wasn't true.

OCTOBER BREAKDOWN

Who knows what happened that morning
you began to grieve, the sadness

of your mother's death suddenly upon you?
Perhaps you looked out the kitchen window,

saw the swing set rusting, the stars painted
on it fading as when night gives

way to morning. Maybe you couldn't find
a bird, knew another winter was too much,

your knuckles swelling with the first snow.
Still, I can't guess what unfastened you,

your thick hands curling around doorknobs,
opening closets like escape routes.

The gray of the sky was nothing new.
It was a coat we put on each October,

an umbrella we hardly knew we held.
But you let go, fell deep

into the hole of yourself. The moons shone
in your fingernails, each one a small lantern.

SQUALL LINE

My mother says the lightning struck
hardest in her backyard and the thunder
seemed to pound on her kitchen window,

like an intruder catching her there,
standing in the light of the open refrigerator.
She wanted to call but couldn't remember

my number, didn't know if it was too late
or too early or if this was even something
she could tell. But this morning

the phone does ring and her small voice
asks where I am, when I can come.
I find her in the yard, picking up twigs and fallen

apples, small wounds the trees shrug off.
I shrug too, wonder if the storm I heard
was just some echo of the storm she knew.

TWILIGHT

When her voice comes into the house,
when her face, that broken watch,
is at my door, all I can think of is
the water I have left running in the kitchen
and the TV, the sportscaster saying
the game is delayed on account of rain.
But she wants to go for ice cream, points
to her bike out front, says we could ride
over. And I think *this is my mother,*
the red face, the hair against her forehead,
the rough fingers on the door handle.
Just for fun she rings the bell, smiles
as the sound ricochets through the house,
travels back to where we stand, the screen
between us. I shake my head, *no,* let her
down easy. But she is slow to leave,
rests against the porch rail, straightens
her hair, finally turns. I watch, hearing
the water again, the TV, as the room
surrounds me and my mother pedals away.

V I G I L

At night I hear my mother's voice,
the sound of rakes scraping
the bare pavement. Outside there is

only the streetlight, rising up
like an awkward votive candle.
Always, I expect to see my mother

standing there, the light buzzing above
her. In the morning the trees admit
nothing, leaves fall past one another,

collect beneath bushes or catch on fences.
The house sits back and the street-
light fades, then goes out, like a wick.

FOGGED IN

1

Fear descends like the fog
on the hills around this valley.

Only nothing seems to burn
them off. No sun here.

2

Everywhere I see my mother
pointing at me, even

the smallest branches, her
fingers, twisted, beckoning:

3

At night she gives me clouds,
keeps stars for herself.

UNDERTOW

My mother walks on beaches.
The sand stretches out before her,

gold and worthless.
She thinks the water makes promises

it can't keep, offers waves
like apologies. They fall

at her feet. The air is thick
with salt, the sting in her eyes.

All around her waves rise up
in anger, whitecaps like rows of fists.

CORRESPONDENCE

I hear your letter panting
in the mailbox, the pale

tongue of a black dog.
The stamp hangs, crooked,

unlucky, my name a stain,
the ink wild with grief.

The postmark could say
anywhere and I'd believe

your pockets are full of sand,
your purse holds small soaps.

The thin pages unfold
in my hands. I lift them

to the light, study the creases.

FOOLISH

I escaped my mother's blue
house to a white one

with blue trim, that little
touch of her. Now she climbs

the hill of the driveway,
comes to sit in my living room,

falls asleep on my couch.
I clip coupons, do anything

to keep busy, to stop hearing
her heavy breathing.

Outside the trees turn
into shadow, the windows

bring in the night, and I
look at my mother's hands,

to ask permission, to feel
the bones, tiny and uneven,

marbles in my palm. But
it is dark when she wakes

startled, her words cracking
wildly in the heat. She has not

meant to sleep here. She
can't imagine why she came.

I want to say, well then leave,
let the screen door slam behind

you, let the porch light burn out.
But she is gone, not even turning

to lift her fingers to the wind,
to let it play them like chimes.

ROOMS BY THE SEA

I

At the end of my bed there is ocean,
the covers dropping off, a jagged

coast. My mother, in another room
in another house, floats, an island,

a thin strip of land barely
anchored down. Our love is

the water between us, sometimes
green, sometimes blue or brown.

II

Hopper was right, opening his door
to the sea. The beach is incidental,

the sand hardly ours. The water
would climb the steps if we let it,

flow right over the floor boards
if we said *come,* if we surrendered.

I I I

O my God, what am I
That these late mouths should cry open
In a forest of frost, in a dawn of cornflowers.
    —Sylvia Plath, "Poppies in October"

FIRST THINGS

I hold the phone, an awkward
shell at my ear. I call
your house to hear the ringing.
Outside rain falls, clumsy,
half hearted. I imagine snow
where you are, the drifts,
countless flakes. A robin
lands on the sidewalk, stands
on one foot, then the other.
He folds his wings behind
him, stares at the brown grass.
The ringing goes on.
The ground holds the grass
close, resists the rain, the bird.
His eyes are dark
with listening, his whole body
waits for the earth to sing.

PRESSURES

Tonight even the wind is small,
beats against the windows like birds
who can't see the glass, ignore
the bricks and mailbox, fly right
through the living room, floor lamps
like strange trees. In the dark
this house is a forest. I leave the door
open, sit on the porch, listen
to the wind fingering the blinds,
searching for leaves or small branches,
something it can move or change.

DISTANCE

As you take cover in a hospital
in northern Michigan, this year's first

tropical storm spins off the shore of Texas
near the town where you spent the winter.

On TV there are empty beaches,
palm trees shaking like wet

fingers over the sink of the ocean.
A thousand miles away, the warning

goes off in you, the startle
of chest pains, the wild strainings.

Today this hospital bed is a beach.
Your children are shells

you'd like to feel in your hands, carry
deep in your pockets. But that

first storm is weak, moving east,
missing land. Far north, the doctors stand

around you, smoothing the sheets
on your bed, calling you lucky.

BIRDS

Birds fly from your mouth,
feathers floating down around you.

Your voice is the quiet between
the flapping of their wings,

white sky, dark bodies.
You speak and they are a curtain

you pull back, wings
closing. You wear them

in bad weather. You hold them,
trembling in your hands.

You sit to write.
Ink drips from their wings.

When you are done, they perch
on your fingertips, find their way

into your pockets. When you sleep,
they tuck their heads in close.

BIRKENWALD

As though he knew Ohio,
the foothills of the southeast,

the trees in fall, wind
sharpened and leafless,

a bag of arrows
carried on the shoulder

of the mountain,
Klimt painted his birches,

the lean muscle of them rising
deep within the forest,

and the leaves below,
colors beneath a pale sky.

WATERCOLOR: DUSK

The fields meet the sky,
both blue in this last

light, the flap of
an envelope closing.

To the left, pine trees
stand, their green shirts

close around them.
In their shadow,

the house, a patch
of light, the yellow

kitchen at dusk,
the many bodies around

the table, or perhaps one
alone, head in hands.